Once Upon A Mail Route

by

John Mooy

Based On A True Story

illustrated by
Wendy Anderson Halperin

EDCO Publishing, Inc.
2648 Lapeer Rd.
Auburn Hills, MI 48326
www.edcopublishing.com

ISBN-13: 978-0-9749412-8-8

ISBN-10: 0-9749412-8-X

Library of Congress Control Number: 2005939153

Printed in the United States of America

MAIL ROUTE STORIES

United States Postal Service

Through the years, the mail has been delivered to many places in many ways; on foot, horseback, stagecoach, bicycle, boat, train, automobile and airplane. Mail also has been delivered by using balloons, helicopters and even pneumatic tubes.

RFD (Rural Free Delivery)

Today it is difficult to recall a time when people living in rural areas did not have a mail carrier stop at their house to deliver mail. In 1893, Postmaster General John Wanamaker, of Pennsylvania, thought mail should be delivered to everyone, even people who lived in the country away from cities and towns. His idea was slow to happen, but in 1896 the first experimental Rural Free Delivery (RFD) routes were started in the West Virginia communities of Halltown, Uvilla and Charlestown. Many people said this new idea would never work. They said delivering the mail to people in rural areas would cost too much money, and it would be too difficult to travel on country roads in bad weather.

But the idea did work, and people living in rural areas, especially the farmers, were very happy to have their mail delivered. After only a few months the Rural Free Delivery was well on its way to becoming an important part of the American way of life. One farmer in Missouri estimated that in the fifteen years he had spent traveling from his farm to the post office, he had traveled nearly 12,000 miles.

The rural mail carrier became a person that could be counted on, as noted in this famous early quote from the ancient Persian people, who had developed their own mail system.

"Neither snow, nor rain, nor heat, nor gloom of night stays these couriers from the swift completion of their appointed rounds."

There are many wonderful stories of mail carriers across America. I know some of those stories because my dad was a mail carrier in Michigan.

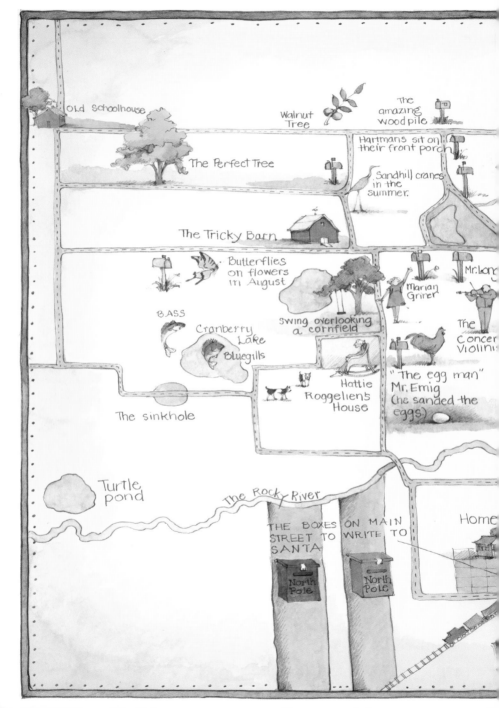

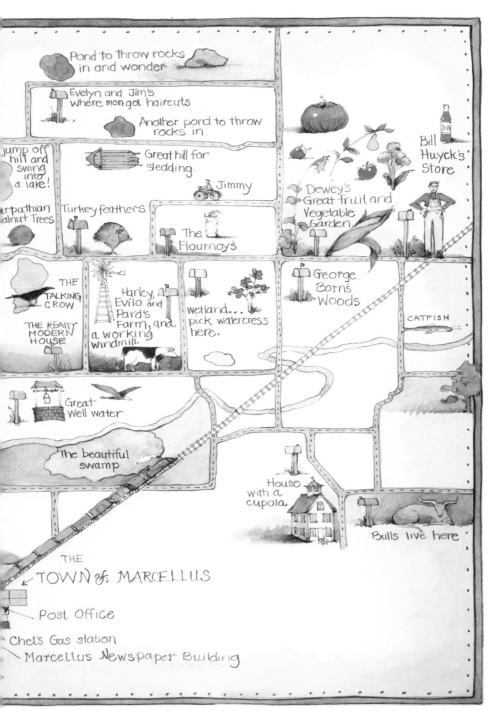

For my Father, Nat, who showed me the beauty of the story by the way he lived his life.

For Wendy, who, after listening to these stories countless times, encouraged me to put them down on paper. And to the pencils, watercolors and imagination she used in creating the illustrations to help bring the stories to life.

For the people in everyday life who "deliver" a kindness to others no matter how large or small.

And to the sound of rural mailboxes being opened and closed.

J. M.

To Jimmy Shannon and the people of Marcellus, Michigan.

W. A. H.

My dad delivered mail for more than 40 years.
During that time he opened and closed
mailboxes nearly 2,680,000 times.
In all these years, he missed less than two weeks
of work. And, as you will see,
he delivered much more than mail.

Once Upon A Mail Route

LOYALTY

The quality or act of being loyal.

If you saw him coming down the road in his car you would know it was my dad right away. He sat next to the window on the passenger side. He had to reach over to steer the car with his left hand, and he used his left foot to push on the gas pedal and the brake. Because no one was directly behind the steering wheel, the car looked a little strange when you saw it coming down the road.

If you waved at him he would stick his arm through the open window and wave back, usually with letters in his hand, and always a smile on his face. It didn't matter if the weather was hot, cold, snowy, sunny or rainy. The window always was rolled down.

Dad worked from the post office in Marcellus, a small rural community located in the southwest corner of Michigan. He drove fifty-one miles on country roads every day, six days a week. His route, by the end of his career, included stops at 219 mailboxes, where he would put mail in, and if the flag on the side of the mailbox was up, he would take mail out. He then drove to the next mailbox, slowing down as he came to each one. Most country roads in Michigan are laid out along section boundaries spaced one mile apart. If there were several mailboxes along that mile-long "block," Dad's car never reached the speed limit.

Dad often would wake me up on Saturday mornings at seven o'clock and ask if I wanted to go on the mail route with him. I always did. I got to sit next to the window and put mail in the boxes.

Dad said there was a story at every stop on his mail route, but I can't tell you all the stories because I usually didn't make it all the way around with him. Dad started and stopped the car so many times that I always would get carsick.

When I got sick only one thing helped.

FRIENDSHIP

Showing kindly interest and goodwill;
Serving a beneficial or helpful purpose.

"Dad, can I get out of the car?"

"Sure, I'll let you off at Evilo and Harley's. I'll deliver the
mail to the end of the road and then come back and pick
you up."

Dad stopped the car in front of Evilo and Harley's
mailbox and I quickly got out. He handed me their mail
and I walked up the gravel driveway that curved around
to the back of their white two-story farmhouse. They
had a dog named Pard. Pard always sat on the porch
by the back door. Before I could go into the house I
had to shake Pard's paw. I liked Pard and we became
good friends.

4

"Hi Evilo," I said. "I don't feel good, so Dad will be back to pick me up in a little while."

"Johnny, I have just the thing that will make you feel better while you're waiting for your father," she said. I pulled out a chair and sat down at the kitchen table. Evilo, (which Dad said is OLIVE spelled backwards) brought me a tall glass of cold milk and a plate that held several of her delicious, homemade, chocolate chip cookies. She then sat down next to me and we talked while I ate. After I finished the milk and cookies I felt a lot better.

I visited Evilo and Harley often because each time I delivered the mail with Dad I seemed to get carsick at about the same place on his mail route.

One Saturday, just after I had finished my snack, Harley, a farmer and a great big friendly guy, came into the kitchen from the barn. He always wore gray bib overalls and a blue work shirt.

"Are you done with those cookies yet, Johnny?" he asked.

"Yes, I am, sir," I nodded.

"Then, let's go to the barn before your dad gets back," Harley said.

When we got to the barn he asked, "Have you ever milked a cow, Johnny?"

"No sir, I haven't," I answered nervously.

Harley then bent over and picked up a well worn, shiny, metal milk stool with three legs and set it on the floor next to the cow . . . toward her backside.

"Well then," Harley said, pointing to the stool "sit down right here, Johnny!"

So I sat down on the milk stool and Harley placed a shiny silver milk pail underneath its udder.

"Go ahead, son, don't be shy," Harley said.

The cow didn't seem to mind all the commotion, so I reached underneath the huge animal as best I could, grabbed her "milk handles," pulled down and squeezed.

Milk squirted into the pail. When the milk hit the bottom of the pail it made a loud, funny, pinging sound. Ping! Ping! Ping!

"Have you ever seen a barn cat," asked Harley.

"What's a barn cat?" I replied.

"A cat that lives in the barn" he said with a laugh.

"Nope," I said.

"Well, just look around, Johnny," Harley replied with a smile.

So I looked around and there were cats everywhere. They were poking their heads from around the corners and between the bales of hay hoping to get a drink of the fresh milk.

Harley laughed and asked, "Why don't you feed those cats, Johnny?"

"I can't," I said, trying to concentrate on what I was doing. "I'm milking the cow."

Harley knelt down next to me and said, "Watch this."

He took the cow's "milk handles," aimed them sideways and squirted milk toward a cat. Pretty soon all the cats gathered around us. They jumped and squirmed as they tried to lick the stream of milk coming toward them through the air. In no time the cats had milk all over their faces and they loved it.

"Better go now," Harley said, after we had fed the cats and finished the milking.

We walked from the barn to the house. Dad was waiting for me in the car. Somewhere between Evilo's cookies and feeding the cats I had forgotten all about feeling sick.

As Dad and I drove down the driveway, Evilo and Harley, with Pard at their side, waved to us from the back porch.

Harley and Evilo were fun to be with. They represented one mailbox and one great time.

GENEROSITY

Freedom in spirit or act; especially, in giving.

It was a gray, rainy, spring afternoon. Dad was walking on our long front porch toward the front door. He had his camera in one hand and a bag filled with groceries in the other. That's the way he always came into the house after work each day. One other thing, he always had a smile on his face.

He walked through the front door, put the groceries and camera on the kitchen table and said with a smile, "You'll never guess what I bought today."

Dad looked at Mom, Mom looked at me, and I was all ears.

Dad began telling his story. "On highway 119 just about a mile south of town a driver lost control of his semi-truck in the rain. The truck skidded on the wet pavement,

jackknifed and overturned. Fortunately, the driver wasn't hurt, but the contents of his truck spilled all over the highway."

"Along with some other stuff," Dad continued, "the truck was filled with boxes and boxes of brand new baseball gloves!"

Dad said according to Michigan law, if a truck tipped over and the contents were spilled, the entire contents had to be sold at a reduced price as "damaged freight." Normally these baseball gloves would sell for over $20, but because of this law they sold for $2 each. What a deal!

"I bought all the gloves," Dad said.

You should have seen the look of surprise on Mom's face when Dad told her we were the proud owners of more than 200 "Larry Sherry" Wilson baseball gloves! (Larry Sherry was a pitcher for the Los Angeles Dodgers who was voted most valuable player in the 1959 World Series.)

Mom had shared plenty of adventures with Dad through the years so she just said, "Now, Nat what are you going to do with 200 gloves?"

"Give them away!" he said.

Dad and I carried all the boxes into the house. Gloves were stacked in the basement, the living room, the playroom and even some behind the table in the dining room. Mom didn't say a thing. She just shook her head and Dad just smiled.

Over the next several months, each morning when Dad left for work he would put several gloves on the backseat of his car, and off he went on his mail route. When children ran out to their mailboxes to greet Dad, he would ask them if they liked baseball. If they answered "Yes," he would reach back, pull out a glove and hand it to them. He came home with lots of stories about how excited the children were and what they said about their "new" gloves.

Sometimes, Dad would just leave a glove in the mailbox. The next day someone would be standing there next to it and ask him if he knew anything about a baseball glove that had showed up in the mailbox the day before.

Dad took particular delight in one mailbox where he "delivered" not one but three gloves for two brothers and their little sister; one for Larry, one for David and the third glove for Margie.

He returned the next day to find a baseball game in progress in the field next to an old red barn. Margie was

at bat, David was pitching, and Larry was in the outfield. When they saw Dad drive up they ran toward his car and gathered around the open, front, side window.

"Looks like you've got a game going," Dad said.

"Yes we do, Nat, and the gloves are just great! Thank you," Margie said.

"Hey, Nat, David and I can catch the ball better than Margie," Larry said.

"Tell Nat the rest though," said Margie in her quiet voice.

"What do you mean?" chimed David and Larry together.

"I can hit the ball farther than the boys," she said with a smile on her face.

"Sounds like you're having fun," Dad said. He continued, "Maybe you can help the boys with their batting and they can help you with your fielding."

The three siblings smiled shyly at one another with understanding.

"I've gotta go now," Dad said, "so batter up!"

He pulled away from the mailbox, and David, Larry and

Margie raced back to their positions and continued their game.

Pretty soon, my dad's great glove giveaway had extended beyond his mail route and into town, until finally, by mid-summer, he had given all the gloves away.

Just down at the end of Elm Street, the street where I lived, was a baseball field. My friends and I would go there almost every sunny day during the summer to play ball.

We'd just slip our gloves over the handlebars on our bikes, ride to the field and choose up teams.

We'd play until it was time to go home for lunch. After lunch, we'd go back to the diamond and play some more until we could hear our mothers calling us home for supper. Our games and those beautiful summer days seemed endless.

As I stood on the baseball field pounding my fist into the pocket of my glove, shouting, "Hey, batter, batter," I would look around and see that my friends and fellow fielders all had the same "Larry Sherry" model baseball glove that I did. We probably were the only town in America where all the kids had the same baseball glove.

I'll bet Larry Sherry would have liked that and this mail route story.

PATIENCE

Bearing pains or trials calmly and without complaint.

There was a story at Hattie Roggelien's house, too, even though she didn't have a mailbox. She didn't need one because my dad went in to see Hattie every single day.

Hattie was 92 years old and nearly blind. She had very white hair, and sat next to an old wood-burning stove in her wooden rocking chair that squeaked every time she rocked.

Every day, before Dad left the post office he called Hattie on the phone to see if she needed anything. He would take her groceries, help her pay bills and read the mail to her. Every Thursday, Dad delivered her copy of *The Marcellus News* and took the time to read it to her.

I liked visiting Hattie. "Come over here and stand by me," Hattie would say. "I want to see how tall you're

getting." When I was standing next to her she would put her hand on top of my head to see if I was any taller than our last visit.

Hattie had two little black-and-white dogs. They were Boston Terriers named Jiggs and Boots. They always wanted me to throw the ball for them to chase. When I did, they would both run full speed across the kitchen floor to get it. It was funny watching them when they tried to stop on the slick linoleum floor.

When one of the dogs got the ball they both would run back to me and keep jumping up in the air, almost as high as my shirt pocket, until I would throw the ball again. This game wouldn't stop until I left the house. The game was fun and Jiggs and Boots loved to play.

The problem was the ball got "slobbery." I always had to wash my hands before we left.

Dad would say, "I'll see you tomorrow, Hattie."

And she would always say, "I'll be right here, Nat."

Sometimes Hattie would laugh and say, "Nat, you're the best mailman I've ever had."

Dad would laugh and reply, "Hattie, I'm the only mailman you've ever had."

Then Hattie would smile, look toward me and say, "Johnny, take two cookies off the plate on the counter for you and your dad."

On our way out, I would take two oatmeal cookies.

And Boots would always bark twice when we left.

You can see why Hattie didn't need a mailbox.

WONDER

Something extraordinary or surprising.

Dad told me he liked his job because every time he went on the mail route it was different. He enjoyed watching the changing of the seasons. I think spring was his favorite time of year. In spring, he watched the new wild flowers pushing up through the earth, the buds on the trees becoming flowers and leaves, the birds migrating from their wintering areas in the South and the frogs and turtles appearing again in ponds and shallow bodies of water after being dormant all winter. Dad said the turtles and frogs would go deep into the pond and snuggle down into the leaves and mud at the bottom, where they would hibernate. He said they could breathe by absorbing oxygen through their skin.

On Cranberry Lake Road we drove by a great pond that I really liked. The pond was round and sat down in a small valley. When Dad stopped the car we could look down the side of the hill into the pond. Starting in early to mid-summer the pond always was very green in color because it was covered with algae. I only know it was algae because Dad told me. It looked like green paint, but he told me that algae were an important source of food and oxygen for other plants and animals in the water.

One morning, Dad stopped the car on Cranberry Lake Road next to the pond. We got out of the car and walked to the edge of the dirt road where we could look down on the green-surfaced water.

"Pick up a good throwing rock, Johnny," Dad said.

I looked around and found a smooth gray rock on the side of the road. It was just a little smaller than a baseball.

"That's a nice one," Dad said.

"Do you think you can hit the center of the pond?" he challenged.

I wound up and let the rock fly. High into the air it went. It flew out over the pond and landed exactly in the middle with a big "KERSPLUSH!"

When the rock hit the water, it caused the green algae to spread out in a circle leaving the water clear in the center.

Magically, the clear circle gradually vanished as the algae reappeared.

It was fun, and didn't hurt a thing. But the next day my arm was a little sore, because Dad let me throw rocks into the pond for a good half hour.

TRUST

Firm belief in the character, ability, strength, or truth of someone or something.

In the southwest corner of Marcellus Township, about half way through the mail route was a very small town called Wakelee. There were a few houses, one small barbershop, a church and a square wooden building that was Bill Huyck's (Hikes) General Store. When we stopped in front of the store and got out of the car we had to take one very large step to get up onto the big cement porch. It was easier for me if I grabbed hold of one of the five wooden posts that held up the porch roof.

When you walked into the store it was amazing. There were tall shelves that went all the way up to the ceiling.

They were loaded with all kinds of supplies from hammers to tires. Bill had "stuff" everywhere. The counters were crowded with cardboard boxes. The floor was stacked with bags of seed corn, reels of wire and rope, shovels and rakes. As you carefully moved your way through the narrow aisles between all the things, the old wooden floor creaked with every step.

Every time I visited Bill's place in winter, I always went to the back of the store, where everybody gathered to sit in the old wooden chairs near the ancient pot-bellied stove. The stove gave off a wonderful warmth and I sat in one of the chairs to dry my gloves and warm my hands.

Bill Huyck, was a tall, skinny fellow who wore bib overalls, work shoes, and an engineer's hat. He always came back to talk to me when I came in with Dad.

"Howdy, Johnny" he would say. "How about a little something to eat?"

"Sure," I would say.

Bill would disappear into the back room and return with a bottle of NEHI® orange soda pop and a white cardboard box filled with raw hotdogs. He would open the box so I could reach in and take out a handful.

I would sit next to the stove and eat the raw hot dogs and drink the orange soda pop. Dad and Bill would stand next to the glass-top counter and talk until I finished. Dad would give Bill his mail and then we would leave the store to finish the mail route.

"Take care of your dad, Johnny" Bill would say as we were leaving.

I never saw Bill any place other than in Huyck's General Store. He liked Dad a lot and trusted him. Sometimes he left cash in the mailbox. Dad would take the cash and put it in Bill's account at the bank in Marcellus. One time he left $32,000 in cash in the mailbox.

Being able to trust somebody is pretty neat.

HOPE

To desire something and expect that it will happen or be obtained.

Just east of Wakelee, down Dutch Settlement Road and just past the mill pond is where Howard and Marian Griner lived. Howard had a short haircut and a smell about him that I liked because he smoked a pipe filled with cherry flavored tobacco.

Marian worked with clay in a studio Howard had built for her right next to the farmhouse. The pottery she made was beautiful. Howard and Marian had nice smiles and pleasant voices and always were happy to see people.

When she was a little girl, Marian's family had been on Dad's mail route, long before she married Howard. Back then, Dad always teased her.

"Hello Mary Ann," Dad would say.

"My name is NOT Mary Ann, it's Marian," she would reply with a laugh.

Dad once told me that when Marian was a little girl, her mother didn't live with them. Marian would write lots of letters to her mom and put them in the mailbox. She always put the flag up so Dad would stop to pick up her letters.

The problem was that Marian didn't have any money to buy stamps. Instead, she just laid some buttons on the envelopes as payment. Dad always picked up the letters and the buttons. Then he would buy the stamps himself and put them on Marian's letters.

I always wondered what Marian wrote in those letters to her mother.

BEAUTY

The qualities of a person or a thing
that give pleasure to the senses.

As the seasons changed, the scenery along the mail route changed too! Sometimes in the spring after a rain, the water in the ponds would be so high it would flood over some of the gravel roads. This made traveling in those areas a bit more difficult and Dad would have to steer the car with both hands. The entire countryside would begin to turn green with new growth and the farmers looked forward to getting their land ready for planting.

On dry summer days so much dust came up behind the car, I couldn't see a thing out the back window until we stopped at a mailbox and the dust settled back onto the road. Dust covered the Queen Anne's lace and everything else growing along the side of the road.

I loved fall because the leaves on the trees were so colorful and the sky always seemed so blue. Flocks of all kinds of birds would gather, getting ready for their trip south. The corn stalks left standing in the fields were a beautiful golden color and the soft breezes through the corn leaves made a gentle rustling sound.

Then winter would come. It could be extremely cold with huge amounts of snow. After a snowstorm the snowplows would push the snow up alongside the shoulders of the roads. The snow sometimes reached so high it was like riding through a narrow white canal. The cold air would blow in through the open window, which made the warmth from the car heater feel so-o-o-o good.

It was easier to put mail in the boxes if I didn't wear gloves. But the metal mailboxes were so cold that as soon

as I put the mail in the box I would cup my hands to my mouth and blow in them to warm them up.

Although the passing scenery on the mail route was different each day, one thing remained the same. It was a very special tree like no other we had ever seen.

It's up here, Johnny, on the right side of the road," Dad said. "I'll stop the car and you see if you can spot it."

No matter what the season that tree was hard to miss, because it was perfect. It didn't have just one trunk like most trees, it had four. Each trunk curved out slightly close to the ground and then went up perfectly straight toward the sky. Amazingly, its branches appeared at exactly the same height on each trunk. And if that wasn't

34

special enough, the branches on each trunk appeared to be identical. It was the marvelous mail route tree.

"I've never seen anything like it," Dad would say. "Mother Nature is something isn't she?"

Dad talked about that tree every time I went with him. He also took pictures of it from exactly the same spot in each of the four seasons.

In time, that tree became another beautiful friend on the mail route.

APPRECIATION

To see the worth, quality or significance of.

George Born was quite a character. He was never home so we never saw him at his mailbox, but he had a story, too.

We never knew where we might run into George. It could be at the gas station, the bank or just about anywhere around Marcellus. When we did meet him he always had on a yellow baseball cap that advertised Hybrid Corn, wire-rimmed glasses, an old, worn, work jacket and blue jeans that were tucked into knee-high, black, rubber boots.

George was an adventurer, so I never knew what he might show me. He had a huge, run-down, old barn filled with just about everything imaginable. He would buy anything from just about anyone. To George, it was like looking for treasures.

One time, Dad took me in the barn where George was
unloading his red, Ford pickup truck. He had rolls of
chicken wire, metal fence posts, and ten, large, cardboard
boxes filled with jars of deodorant. George gave me a jar
of deodorant. It was called "B Sweet." Dad and George
both laughed when he gave it to me.

I always thought it would be fun to be like George. Even
though he was all grown up, he spent much of his time
driving around, exploring the countryside.

One day, Dad and I saw George at the general store.

"Come out to my north meadow and see what I have,"
George said.

We got into George's pickup truck. I sat in the middle
and Dad sat next to the window. George drove down a
muddy, two-track road through the woods. When we got
to an opening in the woods where there was a large
clearing, George stopped his truck.

"Look around, Johnny," George said, "and watch for big antlers."

"Will we see some deer, George?" I asked.

"Nope, now start looking," he replied.

As I looked over to the edge of the woods I saw something moving.

"See'em, Johnny?" George asked.

"Yes! They're huge, George. What are they?"

"They're elk," he said. "Look at the size of those antlers."

We watched and counted eleven elk all together. I had never seen elk before. I wondered where they came from?

"I thought I'd try my hand at elk farming," George said. "It's a lot easier than raising cows . . . why these animals almost look after themselves."

I guess that was why it was so much fun being with George. He was different and liked different things.

You never knew what adventure he might share with you.

ACCEPTANCE

To receive willingly.

Archie Flournoy had a great collection. He collected junk, and he was really good at it because his truck was always full. It was bigger than a dump truck and had high wooden sides.

Archie knew where to get the best junk. He'd find old, broken-down cars and salvage, anything that was made of metal. He'd collect washers, dryers and old refrigerators. If it was made of iron, steel, copper or aluminum, Archie would have it in his truck. Archie sold all his junk to the junk dealer in Three Rivers, a town about fifteen miles away. He sold it by the pound. When he got to the junkyard he drove his truck onto the scales and they weighed it. The junk dealer knew how much Archie's truck weighed empty so when it was weighed full they knew how much metal Archie had collected and how much they had to pay him.

His house and old gray barn sat on a slight hill just off the road. Archie lived there with his wife, Burdine, and two daughters, Cash and Zanet.

On hot summer days Burdine would give me a really cold glass of water or lemonade. I liked the lemonade best because she put the lemons in the pitcher after she squeezed out all the juice. Burdine would always say to me, "Johnny, it's a hot one today, you'd better have another glass of lemonade." I always hoped she would say that.

Archie wore a gray wide-brimmed hat that was stained with sweat because he worked so hard. He also had very strong forearms like my dad. When Archie smiled, he had a small line of gold on his left front tooth that made his smile even more dazzling.

When we would see him on the road in his big truck, Dad and I would wave. Archie would wave back and he always

honked his truck horn. I thought the sound of his horn was just perfect. I loved that sound.

The Flournoys were the first black family I ever knew. They were our friends like everyone else on the mail route.

When Dad retired, his retirement party was held in an old schoolhouse on the mail route. Bucher School was a one-room school house that had been sold to the township. The grass around the school was nicely mowed and several maple trees that had been planted by the students for Arbor Day now towered over the building. A swing set and the backstop for a baseball diamond still stood in the field that once was a playground. The wooden school looked weathered and really needed to be painted . . . but the day was beautiful.

The crowd of people telling stories and laughing brought that old building to life. I stood there looking from one side of the room to the other. I knew some people better than others but Dad knew them all very well.

I had never seen most of them dressed in anything other than their work clothes; but, that day they were in their "Sunday best."

Evilo and Harley were there and so were Marian and Howard. Marian presented Dad with a large, white, ceramic plate she had made. On it she had carefully painted a map of Dad's entire mail route.

George Born was there talking with Bill Huyck who had closed his general store for the afternoon.

Outside the open windows, I could hear a child's voice shouting, "Throw me the ball." This was followed shortly by the sound of a bat smacking a baseball and the unmistakable sounds of children at play.

Archie Flournoy was very ill at the time of the party, but even that didn't keep him from coming. Two strong men carried Archie on a stretcher right up the red cement steps into the school. He was dressed in his best white shirt and tie, brown suit and polished shoes.

"Archie," said Dad as they shook hands, "I'm so glad you're here today."

"Nat," said Archie as he looked up at my dad with that smile, "I wouldn't have missed this for the world."

The people gave Dad a cardboard crown to wear. Spelled out in black letters on the gold-painted crown was "KING OF THE CARRIERS." Everyone looked in Dad's direction as he placed the crown on his head.

The room fell silent. No one knew what to say until Evilo spoke for everyone.

"We love you, Nat."

Everyone in the room stood and applauded. And everyone in the room had tears in their eyes.

Once upon a mail route my dad said to me, "Johnny, there's a story at every mailbox." Because of Dad, I learned that each of the people on his route had their own unique story. Years later, I realized that when Dad took me on the mail route it was because he wanted me to be a part of his own special story.

I now understand I have a unique story, too. My hope is that as I live my own story, I can help make someone else's story a little bit easier and a little bit happier. I know Dad would say, "That's important, Johnny."